MW0117 7958

Once Upon a Time

A Brief History
of All That Was, Is, and Will Be
as Far as We Are Able
to Comprehend

by

Robert John-Patrick Berkeley

DORRANCE PUBLISHING CO., INC.
PITTSBURGH, PENNSYLVANIA 15222

To Bill & Moira,
may the road home always have a
bit of adventure, laughter & much love,
Happy Trails!
Robert & Lourdes Berkeley
Summer
2007

The opinions expressed herein are not necessarily
those of the publisher.

ISBN #0-8059-3984-9
Library of Congress Catalog Card Number
Printed in the United States of America

First Printing

For information or to order additional books, please write:
Dorrance Publishing Co., Inc.
643 Smithfield Street
Pittsburgh, Pennsylvania 15222
U.S.A.

One generation goeth,

and another generation cometh;

and the Earth abideth forever.

Dedication

In honor of my parents,
David and Patricia Berkeley,
and
in memory of my parents-in-law,
Tomas and Luisa Guerzon.

Love
To my wife, Lourdes, whose profession as a dentist reflects her
ability to see the little things that create harmony and beauty.

Insight
To one Father Valerian, a Franciscan who many years ago
instilled in me a love of history and made the past seem
but a brief yesterday.

Example
To all those true humans who struggled with their own times
and strived to make them better regardless of their situation.

Table of Contents

Preface

History and its lessons, as well as its inspiring drama, are all too often lost on the young student and, subsequently, on the befuddled adult. Living in an eternal present, surrounded by a fuzzy future and a muddled past, they stand in the world as ignorant of their coming and going as the most backward of their ancestors. Their understanding of where and when and how and why is often muddled due to an incomprehension as to the sequence of events, as far as they can be known, upon our planet of earthy existence and that which we can ascertain of the existence of our universe.

This book hopes to remedy the situation by bridging the gaps between the founding of the universe, the rise of life and of mankind, the emergence of civilizations ancient and modern, and concluding with a view of where we are going. To live only in the present is to live but a moment. The flavor of the past and the scent of the future can make the fleeting present far richer.

History is all too often incoherent and incomprehensible due to a lack of understanding of the relationship of oneself to the past and to the future. If we can clarify the ignorance of the present by displaying a Map of Time, then the confusion and meaninglessness of the present may somewhat dissipate. The child's and adult's how and why may finally be answered or at least addressed in a logical manner.

Children appear on the scene of life and are all too often not oriented as to where they are in the content of all that has gone before and yet still has an immediate effect upon their present and future. As Einstein theorized, time is relative and, as such, the past, present, and future are all of one. We must overcome this handicap so that all may understand, appreciate, and enjoy the gift of history. A lack of time concept is the major obstacle. Newly dropped into the swaying caravan of life, for far too many the journey makes little sense. Its spirit of growth and accumulated wisdom is lost, for all of which they take note is the camel's rump in front of them.

The questions of where, when, how, and why are often unanswerable due to an ignorance as to the sequence and cause of events, the lessons learned and the contributions made. One fact is meaninglessly piled upon another. The flow of time must be made understandable, otherwise confusion sets in followed by apathy and subsequent ignorance, prejudice, and intolerance.

The premise is that to know the flow of the past is to understand one's present and thus to be able to plan for the future with some guidelines. To not understand the why and wherefore is to be easily misled by those who do. Armed with an understanding of the lessons of the past, future generations may be a bit slower to march off to the trenches and a lot quicker to say no to the aggrandizement of false leadership. An equality of perspective is to be encouraged to avoid the repetitive cycle of mass manipulation which we see even in our own modern, wired era.

We have more of the past and of the future than we do of the present. Our actions and decisions should be informed ones, informed, inspired, and forewarned by the experiences of our fellow human beings who, though they are of the past, have journeyed ahead of us on the road of existence.

Let us now mount the camel, for I think that you will find the view quite spectacular and be amazed at the length of our Caravan.

Part I

The Foundations of the Universe
Current base line date: A.D. 2000
Real time: 15 billion to 4.6 billion years ago

Chapter 1
Once Upon a Time

Once upon a time, there was no time. There was no up and there was no down. There was no east, north, south, or west. As far as our present human consciousness can ascertain, there was no Once Upon A Time.

All that was was. That is to say that it couldn't be if there had never been a be. Or to put it another way, time did not exist and so there was no past, present, or future. No one knows what was going on before time came to be, but whatever it was it was all that there was. Alice in Wonderland would have felt right at home in whatever the situation was before there was the concept of time.

Before our universe came into being, it is possible to consider that there was before time—from our human understanding—a profound nothingness, an unlimited, unbounded void: no sun; no gasses; no stars; no galaxies; no universe; no human mind to comprehend, to question, to ask, to curse, to laugh. There was no light and there was no darkness. There was no here or there. No noise, no silence.

"We were not about," as they say in Australia. Our comprehension of time ends at what we now believe was the beginning of time, matter, and energy—of all that we call the universe.

The state or condition of this nothingness, before the universe was, is not knowable at this point, nor do we have any understanding as to why the universe came into being. We have no scientific or mechanical answer as to why all that is came to be. Theories abound but are as substantive as dreams.

The inquiring mind of Humanity has, through the ages, only been able to climb the wall which separates us in time from the nothingness of no time by speculating, via religion and philosophy, as to who, how, when, where, and why. As death appears to scoff at life, so does the riddle and the mystery of the universe's beginning into Being scoff at our human capacity to know fully of this profound event. We know only that we are, but we do not know scientifically from whence we come nor where we go upon our departure from the seemingly alive.

It is frustrating and yet amusing that we cannot put our human, flesh and blood, minds upon what lay before we came to be and upon what lies ahead after we cease to be. Prideful bursts of knowledge based on ignorance and fear have wrestled with this closed doorknob with little success except to realize that the puzzle of existence is still a puzzle. Ignorance is forgivable, but stupidity, its close cousin, all too often has reigned, in retrospect, as knowledge with horrific results upon the Earth and its creatures. The answers may truly lie only in spiritual speculation and belief. After all, it is a huge universe, and we are discovering that it is also a fantastically large, small universe—via the atom.

Let us return to a level and to a realm which our human intellect can at least begin to reckon with. Let us journey into our conscious, known existence of matter: solid, liquid, gas, and plasma; of bounded space and weight and gravity; of color, light, and sun; of here and there; of big and small; of suns, moons, comets, galaxies, black holes, planets, creatures, humankind, homes, baseball games, hot dogs, school days, tears, and laughter. All that never was before our universe and time, as we comprehend it, began.

And it began with a BIG BANG!

Chapter 2
The Universe Emerges

Our human knowledge—the treasure chest of those individual minds which came before us—has ascertained that our universe began, time began, some 15 to 20 billion years ago with an explosion which occurred at a moment of infinite density. Matter and energy were sent hurtling through what we now call space but which prior to this Big Bang was, as we stated, an unknowable nothingness.

Since there was a nothingness that we can comprehend prior to this emergence of matter and energy, then this gigantic, still-echoing explosion had no center and took place everywhere. Why this astounding event occurred and what happened before this entry of matter and energy is still a mystery. Some scientists have even answered this fascinating mystery of why and what were the nature of the forces which came into existence and the how of their coming to be by simply stating, "Because." This mechanical answer to express our ignorance of the true origins of space, time, matter, and energy is not very satisfactory to even the youngest, budding mind. Let us explore further this—dare we say—creation.

Further development of this Big Bang theory states that a minute, cosmic egg of immeasurable energy exploded. Matter, gravity, and electromagnetism were created and the galaxies, those vast, only recently discovered islands of billions of stars, formed. The universe, right from its first split-second of existence, began to expand at enormous speed, believed in its furthest regions to be expanding at the speed of light.

Tease your brain, your imagination with this thought: if this cosmic egg was all in an infinite, unending nothingness, then was it small or big? We have no way of measuring it since whatever its nature was at that moment, or from wherever or however it came to be, was at that moment all that there was. There was no yardstick of measurement for comparison.

Now we are entering the realm of philosophy and of religion. A further expansion on the Big Bang theory proposes that time may indeed have had an existence before even our universe took shape. This is called the Oscillating Universe theory which proposes that the present universe will continue to expand for another 50 billion years and then gravity will eventually pull the universe back together again, like balls tossed up into the air or a balloon inflating and deflating. Alas, the how and why of it all are still not adequately addressed. Mechanical explanations are limited even when veiled in esoteric scientific jargon.

This "joining together" again will purportedly trigger another Big Bang—the cycle is repeated about once every 80 billion years. All very neat and orderly based on the supposed but unknown mass and volume of the universe. Alas, alas, there is no proof that this can, will, did, or has been occurring, and if there is not enough gravity and mass, then the universe will expand forever. Never mind if there is a who responsible for all of this, but how, why, and what for are not clearly answered except through religious or philosophical constructs. Faith and viewpoints always wrestle with doubt, even when they claim otherwise.

"Just because," is not good enough for most of us. If the universe is to expand forever, it may well be that it will not have sufficient material to reconstitute itself and may at one point simply cease to be. A return to an all-encompassing nothingness will occur. Poof! The Show is over. As of now we are still uncertain about our future.

Prior to the Big Bang and Oscillating Universe theories, there was the now-discarded Steady State theory which propounded a universe with no beginning but an eternal self-sustaining life of birth and destruction and rebirth—change and change again within the universe of matter and energy created from nothing. Here is presented that a universe, despite its origins or lack of them, is perfectly balanced between extinction and existence by the dynamic of constant change. Perfection itself. Who, what, why, and how are somewhat neatly shelved.

To add some clarity to this potpourri of theories, the discovery of radio waves travelling in all directions tends to support the Big Bang theory of a gigantic explosion having occurred everywhere all at once. Everywhere was where it had to be considering that prior to the event, where did not exist. As to the cause, it is unknown.

Our human knowledge, whether it be scientific, religious, or philosophical, can at times appear to be as a dog chasing its tail, never quite arriving at a conclusion. Our origination, that is to say our beginning, and the nature of our past before our beginning is still a mystery, as is our future. The answer may well already lie within our scientific inquiry, our religious faith, or our philosophical viewpoint. As human beings we seem to have a unique trait in that we doubt one another and have been blessed or cursed with a freedom of will which many of us choose to use as the mood strikes us.

Keep in mind that by having analyzed the light from distant galaxies, we believe that the critical distance for the boundary of our observable universe is about 15 billion light years from Earth. Any galaxy receding from us at the speed of light will never be seen by us or detected by us. So there is that which we can see and that which we will never see. And what lies beyond that which we can never see? Ah, another mystery!

But enough of these mysteries. We know that we are part of a young, 15 billion-year-old universe with a possible 60 billion years of existence left. Let's move on to explore our own backyard in our galaxy, the Milky Way, in our own cozy solar system, and on our planet Earth.

While the universe is our space and time, the Earth is our current Home, and the sun its source of warmth and light and life. Let's go home, for our mere being, our existence, in conjunction with our sun, solar system, and galaxy, is as mysterious and as improbable as is the beginning of the universe and time—as we humans judge it. We are children of the universe with our own address.

Chapter 3
Our Sun, Our Earth

The Milky Way galaxy in which our sun/star resides, along with some 100 billion other sun/stars, was formed from the Big Bang. Its formational age as such is not known except that it is, as an entity, far older than our sun.

The sun, our sun, our star, is an insignificant yellow dwarf star which lies some 32,000 light years from the center of our galaxy. It takes our solar system approximately 225 million years to complete one journey around the center of our galaxy.

It has been estimated that our sun is approximately 5 billion years old with perhaps another 5 billion years of life left. There is still plenty of time left to do your laundry and to complete your homework. The sun is big enough to contain more than a million earths. It is principally made up of hydrogen and helium constantly exploding across its diameter of 864,950 miles.

If our sun were much larger or smaller than it is, life on Earth could not exist. We would be either fried or frozen. Had it been twice its size— and some stars are fifty times the size of our sun—it would have burned itself out already. If it had been smaller, it would have given out so little heat that our Earth would be in a permanent freeze and far, far too cold for any life to have happened or to have survived. We are placed just right at 93 million miles from a just-right star. Lucky us.

Toward the end of its life, some 5 billion years from now, our dear sun will swell up into a terrible Red Giant star that will engulf and swallow up the planets Mercury, Venus, Earth, and Mars. Eventually, our planet Earth and our bones shall become one with the sun.

The important point to remember is that our sun is fortuitously placed to supply us with just the right amount of radiant heat to promote life and survivability upon our planet as we whirl through space. Our sun is middle-aged at 5 billion years old, and we reside with it on an outer arm of our galaxy, which was formed some 15 billion years ago. So, our sun is a relative newcomer of formed matter of a reality that we can somewhat comprehend.

Now let us examine our own planet Earth, the third planet from the sun in the galaxy Milky Way. We are the Blue, Watered planet, the oasis of our solar system, our current residence, Earth. Despite your nationality or race, you and I, all of us who call ourselves humans, are Earthlings.

About 4 billion 6 hundred million years ago, our Earth was formed by the same force that pulled the solar system together. Gravity, the force which was created at the time of the creation, pulls objects together. Gravity pulled a large cloud of dust and gas into a spin, increased perhaps by the explosion of a nearby star, a super nova. Eventually, gravity pulled bits of cloud and gas together into larger and larger clumps with the largest becoming the sun and the rest becoming the planets and other objects such as the moons and asteroids. Our solar system was formed whirling around our sun.

Our Earth is believed to have formed as an entity some 400 million years after our sun, making us the inhabitants of a 4 billion 6 hundred million-year-old planet. At that time, our Earth would not have been recognizable to us. Indeed, there was no life and no Earthlings either. Life would not emerge from the forming ocean soup of the Earth for approximately another 3 billion 6 hundred million years. We shall cover the emergence of life very shortly, but it is important to realize that we are creatures born billions of years ago from a primordial soup of dust and gas. We are made of stardust.

Our Earth lay a-forming for over a billion years; blessed by its position and the tilt of its axis from our sun, an oasis of life was forming in the dark void of the exploding, expanding universe. This dot in the Firmament was and continues to be the home of life forms in abundance and of one form that will eventually wonder and marvel and question its very existence with a reverberating, "how, why, when, where, who, what for?"

Our Earth's existence is tied to the sun's life, as we stated, for when the sun dies, our Earth will once again become part of the dust and gas of the universe. Perhaps this explains our restlessness. It has even been speculated that life itself came from elsewhere and just found a planet that was hospitable to its growth and development. In turn, we too shall perhaps journey to other worlds despite our current limitations. Our dreams often do lead to our accomplishments.

What of humankind? Well, before we speculate further on our possible future let us see how we arose and when, for we must know of our past before we can speculate upon our future. We must know of what we are and of the nature of our legacy.

Part II
The Rise of Life and Humankind
Current base line date: A.D. 2000
Real time: 3 billion 600 million
to 35,000 years ago

Chapter 4
The March Begins

For a billion years, our planet was an empty stage of rock, molten lava, and rain. An atmosphere had formed and the stage was being readied for the grand Parade of Life in the darkness of space.

To gain an understanding of this vast scale of time, scientists, from studies of the Earth's crust, have distinguished four broad geological eras since the Earth began. To simplify an understanding, we shall deal with the four epochs/eras and not the numerous subdivisions or periods within the four eras.

The first era is called the Precambrian. This is the longest period and the least understood. Approximately 87 percent or roughly 4 billion years of the Earth's history occurred during this era. Millions of years passed during this period then the rock crust of the Earth cooled. Later the oceans formed, as did the atmosphere surrounding the Earth. Simple single-celled life forms developed after a billion years in the oceans forming algae and bacteria. The oldest fossil remains are of tiny thread-like cells in some rock formations of western Australia. They have been carbon dated to 3 billion 6 hundred million years ago. The universe was working its magic upon the little blue planet.

The second era is called the Paleozoic. This era began some 600 million years ago and lasted for about 375 million years. During this time, more complex sea life developed, such as sponges and snails. Before the era ended 225 million years ago, the first land plants appeared, as did the first animals, such as amphibians and reptiles. Life was now not only in the ocean but was moving out to live upon the land. The Earth was becoming a busy place.

The third era is called the Mesozoic. This era began some 225 million years ago and lasted for about 160 million years. It ended about 65 million years ago. Life on land reached abundant and grotesque-to-us proportions. The climate during this period was generally mild. Small animals, the mammals and birds, first appeared. Most insects, such as flies, ants, termites, and moths, came to be. Snakes, lizards, alligators, and turtles—all reptiles—entered the parade. This age was dominated by the dinosaurs, the dominant species. These gigantic creatures ruled the Earth for close to 160 million years. No larger creatures have ever lived on land. Some weighed fifty tons.

There is a theory that the dinosaurs disappeared due to the collision of the Earth with an asteroid. Unusually high amounts of the rare element Iridium have been found in the Earth's crust dated to about the time that the dinosaurs suddenly became extinct. The smashing into Earth of a huge asteroid or asteroid shower would have darkened the sun's light for a sufficient time to break down the food chain, thus destroying the dominant species of giants.

One other major event happened during this era. The unified land mass of Pangaea began to break up and drift off across the surface of the Earth forming the continents as we now know them. This process is ongoing. Note how neatly South America fits into the coastline of Africa.

As of yet no primate, ape, or human being yet walked upon the Earth, despite the passage of three geological ages and some 4 billion 535 millions years of Earth's existence. Approximately 98.5 percent of all time on Earth had passed, and humankind was nowhere to be found. The life force has its own timetable and agenda.

With the demise of the dinosaurs came the birth of the Fourth era and of Humanity. Let us hope that is not a "saving of the best for last." The Cenozoic era is the fourth era in which we now reside. This era began some 65 million years ago and has lasted to our present day. Land forms that we see today developed in the Cenozoic. The climate late in this era became much colder than during the Mesozoic era. Several ice ages took place where huge sheets of ice covered great expanses of land. Their last retreat from North America, Europe, and Asia occurred only about 35,000 years ago. Large mammals appeared that could live in the extreme cold, such as the elephant-like woolly mammoth. Flowering plants, hoofed animals, and the primates appeared.

From this vast expanse of 65 million years, we as a species of life have appeared, have evolved, have come to be. Yet our written history is but some 6,000 years old. We are but newcomers on the stage of life upon the planet Earth. Let us now explore the unknown and known history, the story of the rise of the now-dominant species of life on Earth, the story of Humanity of which you and I are a part.

Chapter 5
Man-Apes

Some 65 million years ago, a branch of the mammal line of warm-blooded creatures which had developed during the latter part of the Mesozoic era some 15 million years previously developed into the primate. It was not until some 12 million years ago that the first hominid, a member of the family Hammond which includes ape-men and humans, emerged from the primate line of apes. Ramapithecus was a small ape-like creature and may well be the earliest hominid. The hominids were not apes. It is believed that in order to survive the climatic changes, certain apes had adapted to living on the ground. There their circumstances changed, and they became something other than that which they were.

The hominids are thought to be the direct ancestors of modern man. They gradually evolved into forms which were more man-like in appearance and which possessed certain of the superior qualities of modern man, such as a powerful opposing thumb and forefinger which could be manipulated easily, thus making the hand a great asset; a more highly developed brain and nervous system; good vision even at close distances; erect stance; the ability to talk and, thus, to communicate with his fellows; and the ability to fashion and use tools to aid him. This was a creature who was clearly stepping out of his confined behavioral patterns and was about to strike out on his own.

The next tentative step in evolution toward our development as modern man was the homonid Australopithecus, a hominid who could walk on two legs some 5 million years ago. His face had some human features. Neither fire nor the wheel was as yet used or invented. Skeletal remains of hundreds of australopithecines have been found in eastern and southern Africa. Our knowledge is constantly evolving as to our ancestors, and evolving also means discarding past knowledge. Truth is a tricky item. We are not certain as to where hominids originated, for there is strong evidence for origination upon the African continent. There is also debate and some evidence of spontaneous generation over the Earth. Time will tell—perhaps.

It is difficult to decide whether these ancestors of the past were really men and women. They used primitive tools but so do chimpanzees. Yet, from our lofty perspective, science senses that we are akin to them. New discoveries and "missing links" are constantly being discovered and theorized. The fact cannot be denied that these ancient beings are our rough cousins, though we may esthetically disapprove.

We can at times hardly understand ourselves or our fellow humans. Our own motives and actions at times are a mystery of incomprehension. Their legacy of experience runs through our own genes from the dawn of our coming to be. Their increased brain capacity did aid in their survival, but their frailty in the face of nature and their ability to survive must give us pause.

Chapter 6
Neanderthal, Cro-Magnon, and Homo Sapien

Slightly more than 2 million years ago, the first man-like creatures developed called Homo erectus. This individual had no chin but could walk upright. Homo erectus made use of fire and produced tools, including the first true hand ax. They built huts, bows, and weapons. They had rudimentary speech. They buried their dead and, indeed, may have had a belief in an afterlife. Burial sites have been discovered in China and have been dated to 400,000 years ago. Europe, Asia, and Africa were now being occupied. Homo erectus had given thought to his and her existence and experience.

From 1.5 million years ago to 10,000 years ago (8000 B.C.) the Ice Age occurred. This was also called the Paleolithic period. Four long periods of glaciation occurred during which the polar ice caps expanded across the continents. Each of these glacial periods lasted around 40,000 to 60,000 years and were separated by warm periods which lasted some 40,000 years.

Many people and animals died during these harsh times, but humanity continued to develop and to use its brain power to adapt and to survive. They were hunters and gatherers, and they stood by one another.

During this period, about 100,000 years ago, the first fully human beings developed, Homo sapiens neanderthalensis, called Neanderthals. Neanderthals evolved and for a while existed among the later Cro-Magnon and Homo sapien/modern man until some 40,000 years ago. He closely resembled modern man but was short, about 5'4"; had a large head and face; and had heavy eyebrow ridges. He made tools of flint and was an excellent hunter. He buried his dead with flowers. Across the ages, this poignant act can still touch our hearts. This alone was further evidence of mankind's growing intellect and questioning of earthly existence.

No one knows why Neanderthal man disappeared. He may simply have died out, but it is more likely that he was absorbed through mating by Homo sapiens/modern man. Nonetheless, our friend with the squat physique and the heavy eyebrows was one of us.

An early breed of Homo sapiens/modern man was Cro-Magnon man whose fossils have been found at 60,000 years ago. He was tall, slimmer than Neanderthal, and had a larger brain similar to Homo sapien/modern man. He was more sophisticated than his Neanderthal cousin.

Cro-Magnons painted upon the walls of caves, further expressing their inner life. This points to an important development, an early need to go beyond the physical, to connect the physical world with beauty, sentiment, and the spiritual. Speech developed. Crude religions developed, as did the beginnings of trade. Deeper stirrings were occurring within the minds of our precursors which were and still do lead to our inspiration and our degradation.

It was not until about 35,000 years ago that our own completed form of Homo sapien/modern man walked forth from the ranks of the Neanderthals and Cro-Magnon people. In the context of time upon the Earth, we are as a class of humanity here but a moment ago. Our brief time to date has been a very busy one. Some would say a bit too busy.

The Mesolithic period lasted from 8000 to 6000 B.C. (10,000 to 8,000 years ago). This period was marked by the dominance of Homo sapiens and a greater degree of culture with notable improvements in hunting and fishing. We were eating better, though life was to our modern view incredibly harsh.

The Neolithic period lasted from 6000 to 4000 B.C. (8,000 to 6,000 years ago). This period was marked by the development of agriculture; the domestication of animals; migration; home construction; invention of the wheel and axle; superior stone tools; and home crafts, such as weaving and spinning. Now we were really moving. Change moved on at a quickened pace.

Humanity was now fully upon the world, progressing materially, adapting to the environment, and communicating ideas through speech to his fellows and to his children. For close to 4.498 million years, counting from Homo erectus who was probably the first pre-human to learn how to actually start a fire and cook with it (no easy accomplishment), the Earth had gotten along quite well without us hominids or humans or whatever we call ourselves. We are a busy, inquisitive lot, a hardy lot. We have endured glaciers, famine, disease, and each other, as well as our own individual turmoils. Life was no bowl of cherries, but no other creature was more able, more tenacious, or eventually more feared even amongst themselves.

At 20,000 B.C. (22,000 years ago) there were probably not more than 10 million humans in all the world compared to our nearly 7 billion today. Busy creatures indeed. Yet we as a species from 2 million years ago have been here less than 1 percent of the Earth's existence. As babes in the wood, we dominate the Earth as no creature has before, for good or ill. We have accomplished this by creating civilizations. So let us begin to examine our political, civilized history. It is quite a story.

Part III
The Emergence of Civilizations
Current base line date: A.D. 2000
Real time: 6,000 to 1,500 years ago
(4000 B.C. to A.D. 476)

Chapter 7
Western History/Ancients and Civilizations

Exhausting journey, isn't it? We have travelled some 4,599,994,000 years since our planet formed. We can feel comfortable enough to say that humankind began in earnest to differentiate themselves from nature and began to control events in the world through bonding, organization, and unified behavior. History began its glorious and tear-filled march by being written down, by passing on its events, by teaching us of the good and bad of which humankind is capable. It is hoped that we learned from our predecessors, but that has not always been the result.

All well and good, but history, that is the written record of humankind's triumphs and tragedies which was for the most part obscure and blank, began to form only about 4000 B.C. or about 6,000 years ago. Not much of a history when we remember that Homo sapien/modern man has been around for some 35,000 years.

You may well be asking yourself, "What is B.C. and A.D.?" In order to date events by years, we number them from a prominent event. Different people use different years or events from which to begin counting their history. The Greeks counted from their first Olympiad. The Romans counted from the founding of their city of Rome. We and the world today use the birth of Jesus Christ as the common era to avoid world-wide confusion on yearly dates.

If we decided to use Roman time using the founding of the city of Rome in 753 B.C., that is 753 years before the birth of Jesus Christ, then we would simply add our 2,000 years (A.D.) since Christ was born to the 753 years since Rome's founding, thereby giving us a Roman year of 2753.

The computation of time before Christ's birth is all B.C. (Before Christ). This is approximately 15 billion years of time. From Christ's birth, we count forward to A.D. 2000, and from Christ's birth we can count backward into time, so that Rome was founded in 753 B.C. or 753 years Before Christ (-753). Our Earth time is far, far longer. Christ's birth is but a convenient break in the flow of our 4.6 billion years as a planet and to begin a new era from a fixed point in history. It avoids confusion and unites us in a time frame.

Civilization comes about when people learn how to write, live in heavily populated areas, are economically dependent on one another, expand their trade connections, develop a powerful government, and advance in arts and sciences. Our first evidence of this occurred almost simultaneously in the Tigris-Euphrates Valley (Mesopotamia in the Middle East) and in Egypt. Only much later did true civilization begin in India, China, and Europe.

For convenience' sake we have divided history into Western and Eastern. It is still the written story of our past from which humankind can learn the complex patterns of human development from the earliest to recent times. History focuses on civilizations which are not necessarily good or bad but are attempts by certain groups of Humanity to organize their existence.

To review our points of time, remember that the history of the world, which is at times forced upon you in school, is only some 4,000 years from the Sumerians and Egyptians, plus another 2,000 years since Christ was born. We have but a rough idea of just 6,000 years of human history out of the 4 billion 6 hundred million years of Earth's existence; of man-like hominids 12 million years ago; of the first men 2 million years ago; of Neanderthal men 100,000 years ago; of Cro-Magnon man 50,000 years ago; and, finally, of Homo sapien/modern man 35,000 years ago. We can but begin an approximate, formal study of civilization, of history, only to 6,000 years ago.

All that went before is mostly lost in time, in miscellaneous artifacts, bones, tools, speculation, and the conjecture of anthropologists. Sheer survival was what absorbed humanity for 2 million years, not the recording of his comings and goings, of his thoughts and relations. The world was an uncivilized, harsh place, and we still carry much of this legacy in our genes despite the civilizing effect of the past 6,000 years.

In our genes we do carry much of our human legacy, more so than in our sanitized history books. We know so little of our long yet short walk upon the Earth. So many are gone as if they never were, yet the collective human consciousness and gene pool reflects the saga and struggle of those comrades of long ago.

Let us begin with what we do know of the Western ancient world which has its roots in Mesopotamia some 6,000 years ago or 4000 B.C. We shall place in time the main Western civilizations of the Sumerians, Egyptians, Persians, Greeks, and Romans. This is not to say that other cultures did not arise during this period, but these were the dominant cultures for their moment of time in history. Nor do we mean that they were morally or intellectually superior; history teaches a hard lesson that the center stage of might and power does not always belong to the righteous or to the just, indeed it can be quite the contrary.

Chapter 8
Sumerians and Egyptians

Between the Tigris and the Euphrates Rivers, in what is now modern-day Iraq, rose the first civilization called the Sumerians. With a constant water supply, fodder for their animals, food for themselves, and building material for homes from season to season, there was no reason to wander and search for survival. So at 6,000 years ago or about 4000 B.C., planning and organization replaced wandering for one group of humans. Ruler and ruled became the norm as organization provided rules, and rules provided benefits for all, more or less, much like today.

City-states arose and developed considerable power based on flourishing agriculture with irrigation. Pottery and metallurgy were made into fine art allowing for storage and organized, armed protection. The Sumerians began cuneiform (tablet) writing, providing for contracts and expanded trade along with the concepts of legality and trust.

These were tremendous advances which served to insure the future and extend the daily horizons of humanity. No longer were these people bound to forage on a daily basis for food, shelter, and water but could now plan, project, and hope for an improved life and more leisure to think of better, more efficient ways to safeguard their earthly existence or just get into trouble.

Alas, the Sumerians were not to last forever. They were to be not only the first civilization but also the first of many civilizations to rise and fall as the leaves fall from the trees. Civilizations seem to collapse due to internal rot or a combination of internal and external causes; like light bulbs, they grow dim and go out.

Soon enough other groupings of humans came, saw, and conquered. War has been the constant companion of humanity, destroying what once was, yet often replacing the old with a virile improvement upon the bones of the departed. "Sic transit mundia gloria," "So passes the glory of the world." Every civilization appears to have an overriding positive and negative trait. It may well be that each carries within it the seed of its own growth and ultimate end.

Organization, custom, tradition, government, law, and religion were concepts being honed to a finer and finer edge by each succeeding group. There was no going back to disorganized wanderings. Regimentation and hierarchy were replacing the old freedoms of the hunters. Survival was becoming easier and more complex. Complexity, while leading to improvements in the use of resources, also led to levels of confusion which internally allowed external and internal forces to bring an end to the civilization. The balancing act between freedom and cohesion, regimentation and liberty, justice and expediency, morality and license, duty and dishonor is not an easy act to carry from one generation to another.

The Sumerians were the first to flourish and to write of their passing, and the first notable civilization to fall as each conquest replaced old rulers and ruling classes with new races such as the Elamites, the ferocious Assyrians, the Chaldeans, the Syrians, the Hittites, the Medes, and the Persians. All have had their day in the sun of the Fertile Crescent, the Cradle of Civilization. Each brought forth their good and their horrific, for the history of these times is similar to our own—a time of progress, horrible bloodshed, and treachery, glorious and tragic. As a species, we mean well; it just does not always come out the way we mean it to be. We contend with cooperation and conflict; we love and mistrust; we seek life, we kill.

Nonetheless, from this time onward Humanity strove and struggled with its ignorance and arrogance to enhance and to improve itself from one generation to the next—not always successfully. The frail torch of communication and lessons learned has been passed via history onward to you. From this region we gained writing, contracts, government, and from the Babylonian city king Hammurabi, a code of laws introducing a concept of justice and fairness for the evils men do to one another.

Let us now cross westward across the Sinai to the land of the Nile.

About 5,200 years ago or 3200 B.C., the Egyptians emerged as a unified civilization at approximately the same time as the Sumerians and for similar reasons. Egypt had one advantage, it was her desert which protected the Nile valley from invasion (for a while) from the East and the West.

The history of this ancient land is long and varied, covering some 2,868 years of official history as a mover and shaker of our Earth. Conquered, resurgent, and conquered again, the Egyptians nonetheless have left us with a unique gift and a breakthrough in attitudes and thought to which much of the human race still holds on today. They kept pace with the Sumerians but contributed one more item to the treasure box of civilization: a unique religious, spiritual dimension that took the consciousness of Humanity beyond its frail, troublesome physical limitations. They optimistically introduced the concepts of hope and expectation via religion and luxury.

A whole world view is involved in appreciating the meaning and role of religion in ancient Egypt. Each year the Nile pulsed, sweeping away the past and making new the land. Its steady cycle was ever recurring, changeless, the embodiment of a cosmic rhythm. The supreme change which threatened mankind then and now is death. Death, the greatest expression of decay and flux which is the common experience of all. Death seems to make all of life a cruel joke. Under the Egyptians it was put into a perspective that offered not a final end but a gateway to a new beginning, to a changeless more perfected realm for all of mankind.

Sensing that this life was not perfect even within the regimented security of civilizations and that their hearts and minds aspired to perfection, the Egyptians devised a religious outlook, a belief. Through ritual and symbol, through preparation and moral worth, whether he or she be a pharaoh or a commoner, one could aspire with reasonable confidence to achieve changeless well-being in an afterlife. Unlike the gloomy version of the Mesopotamians, mankind could be happy and happier still beyond the confines of the mortal body, beyond this Earth.

This heroic, optimistic ethic which induced a view of the nature of the cosmos lifted Egyptian civilization into the pursuit of the best of life, of seeking joy and prosperity. To have joy and contentment in life and to bring it into the world beyond was a driving force in the nature of their civilization. Life was no longer viewed as a mad scramble for fleeting power and wealth but as a journey and a preparation.

The use of religion would be used through the ages to manipulate and to strike fear into the hearts of the ignorant, but the concept of a higher realm open to all men of good will could not be put back into the bag. Death was no longer viewed as an end but as a beginning once one's life had been completed upon Earth.

The introduction of papyrus paper and the building of the Pyramids (3200 B.C. to 2200 B.C.) are but frosting on the cake of Egyptian ideas and innovations. Their art, attitude, and politics, at their best, call to us as kindred spirits seeking answers to the whys of human existence. Their minds addressed the large issues of living a life and of mortality.

In their long history they also suffered periods of decline and decay, of conquest and of being conquered by the Amorites, the Hyksos (1500 B.C.), the Nubians (712 B.C.), the Assyrians (600 B.C.), the Persians (525 B.C.), Alexander the Great in 332 B.C., and finally the Romans in 31 B.C. ended their independence in the ancient world.

Death and Rebirth were a constant theme in Egypt and in the world as they viewed it. They held forth and fast to a belief in harmony and a universal justice beyond the mortal world. Despite the chaotic nature of humanity they discerned that humans were prepared for perfection, that the ideal in their hearts was their truer self.

This influence was sharpened by the Hebrews (1900 B.C.), 3,900 years ago. After fleeing Egypt in 1300 B.C. under their leader, Moses, they became a nation with a national God; the One God of Israel imbued them with a devotion to ethical righteousness and the One God that has never been lost. The concepts of morality and the God of Israel were established as powerful and permanent parts of the Western heritage.

This one thread of a world beyond, of ethical justice and concern, inspiring and guiding human nature and actions owes its debt to the Egyptians and the Hebrews. The human race acts contrary and other religions and political views have risen against these optimistic views of the nature and purpose of existence, yet after some 6,000 years we still have found so little else that can guide us with honor, dignity, and hope as we walk through the mud below and gaze outward to the stars.

Chapter 9
Persians

Upon the flux and flow of Mesopotamian nations arose the Persians some 2,612 years ago (612 B.C.). They conquered the cruel Assyrians and extended their own empire from Egypt and Judea into modern Turkey and east to the frontiers of India. The extension of their rule far dwarfed any previous nation's expansion from the Fertile Crescent.

The Persian Empire was to last about 289 years and was founded on the might of the Persian army and by setting the precedent of respecting and adopting the best of the higher cultures which they conquered. Harsh militarism was not the method by which they governed and subjugated their diverse population. Although the emperor was in theory an absolute monarch, power rested on a policy of toleration and decentralized power wielded by various administrative officials. It worked, for rebellions were rare, a "world state" atmosphere was encouraged.

The Persians concentrated on enjoying a luxurious existence supported by tribute from the empire. Peace and commerce prevailed, if not political freedom. Stability was ensured by the might of the army and the benevolent treatment of the varied conquered peoples.

The primitive mythology of the Persians was transformed into an ethical religious system by the prophet Zoroaster, who preached that the world was torn by the contest between good and evil, between God and the Devil. Man was required to choose because he was faced eventually with a last judgement that would result in the destruction of the wicked.

As we may note, the flowering of our Christian faith has been built upon the ideas of justice and righteousness of the Egyptians, Hebrews, and the Persians, as well as the cosmic views of the Far East as we shall see. It appears that the Persian Empire served as a bridge of thought and commerce between the East and the West. The mind of humanity was not only concerned with power and trade but with questions of the spirit.

Despite the political domination of the ancient civilizations of the Near East, Persia was to flounder and break upon the spears of the Greeks and to finally go under the domination of Alexander the Great and his Macedonian/Greek cohorts in 322 B.C. (2,332 years ago). It seems that success brings about decay and spinelessness, for the shattering of the might of Persia by the "barbaric" Greeks came as a shock to the Eastern psyche. From its destruction the balance of power shifted westward to Greece and then, to close the final chapter of the ancient world, to Rome.

The ancient civilizations of Sumeria, Egypt, Babylonia, Hittite, Assyria, and Persia, despite their impressive achievements, failed to present us with a picture of progressive political development. We see one mighty potentate succeed another without much change in the essential pattern of a society dominated by an elite of royalty, generals, and priests. Nonetheless, their art, language, administrative ability, commerce, and spiritual development were to leave lasting contributions to the Western tradition. The basis of a future world civilization which would encompass more and more individuals was in the making.

The 6,000 years of recorded history of civilization from the Sumerians (4000 B.C.) to our own age (A.D. 2000) was reaching its midpoint by 1200 B.C. (3,200 years ago) when a new people entered the scene of history from the wilds of Europe and put an end to the world dominated by the ancient peoples of the Middle East. The Greeks now marched forth with a very different tune, one which reverberates into our own time and world view: "Citizen, what do you think?"

From the Middle East we have learned to speak, to write, to have trade, to administer, to wage war, to govern, and to dwell upon the meaning of our activities from an ethical and spiritual viewpoint. No other creature upon this Earth has ever done as much.

Let us now journey westward to Europe.

Chapter 10
Greeks and Alexander the Great

As we have done with the Birth of Christ, so the Greeks before Christ used their first Olympian games in 776 B.C. to count their years. This was fine, though they as a people had occupied Greece for some 300 years before the first Olympics, in 1176 B.C. (3,176 years ago).

The Greeks presented a different ideal and a startlingly different perspective to civilization. Perfection in mind and body, as embodied by the Olympics, went hand in hand with their ideal of mental and spiritual development for all citizens. The best of their civilization displayed an ideal of individual growth and introspection, not just a preparation for another world beyond but a perfection of life in this world. Their civilization sought a working out of thought to answer the doubts, fears, and hopes of those who seek out what it means to be fully human in the world.

Philosophy, and some have said psychology, were born alongside the birth of the Western ideal of democracy, no longer merely ruler and ruled, monarch and subjects, but fellow citizens. This change in attitude toward the people of the state was personified in the city-state of Athens. Here Greek art, science, mathematics, and philosophy reached their full flower, leaving us of the West with a legacy of individual dignity and responsibility which has set us apart from the autocratic rulers of the Fertile Crescent.

Unable to overcome their fierce independence, Greece was never united during this time as a nation. They nevertheless showed their steely determination to do things their own way by twice defeating invasions from Persia between 490 to 479 B.C. These victories, while temporarily uniting the Greek city-states, led to contention between the two most prominent cities of Sparta and Athens. Unable to resolve their differences, their civil war—the Peloponnesian War—led to the eventual weakening of Greece and its subjugation by Philip of Macedonia and his son Alexander the Great, both admirers of Greek culture and thought.

29

Despite the eventual conquest by the Macedonians, the Athenian democracy of 450 B.C. succeeded because it possessed and transmitted through education to its citizens a set of ideals that allowed its people to cooperate and to decide great issues wisely. Democracy and the worth of the individual, the educated citizen was a concept not easily put away. The spirit of individual inquiry was loosened upon the world, "Hey, you know what I think..."

One other critical lesson learned from the Greek experiment which was not repeated until the American Revolution of A.D. 1776, 2,226 years later, was that freedom also allows one to go to hell in one's own way. Thus the lesson of history in Greece is a beginning with a golden-aged democracy declining into ease and a decayed imperialism of its own; democracy requires vigilance and education and idealism.

In 322 B.C. (2,323 years ago) Alexander the Great of Macedonia, after defeating all of the Greek city-states except Sparta, began his conquest of the then-known world with the exhortation, "We are free men, they are slaves." He smashed the Persian Empire in a series of campaigns beginning in 334 B.C. and went on to found the largest empire known at that time, which included Asia Minor, Syria, Palestine, Babylonia, Persia, and Egypt. He had an international concept of unifying the world under one civilization founded upon Greek thought. He sought to fuse the cultures of the East and the West via intermarriage and unified armies of varied nations going forth "to know the unknown."

On his armies' journey to the East, to the frontiers of India, he had established numerous cities which became centers of Greek trade and culture. He made the attempt to spread the best of liberating Greek thought throughout the known world. Because of his personality, his unlimited power, and his military invincibility, Alexander seemed the personification of world empire and, unlike the Persians, his concept of such an empire fostered the idea of a universal citizenship, and not of benign subjugation.

The movement toward world empire which Alexander had initiated would continue throughout history. Sadly, upon his early death at age thirty-three in the year 323 B.C. (2,323 years ago), his empire broke into pieces, through it did not forsake its Hellenic heritage. There was desperate, frequent warfare; considerable cultural progress; commercial trade; and a flourishing of the art of government. The world had become a more open, inquiring place, despite the resumption of the Oriental form of absolute royal rule. An intellectual community had been created which no government could control and which allowed an exchange of ideas between East and West. As a result, not only trade but the ideas of Christ, Buddha, and Muhammad with their message of social concern and universal salvation moved across the world and acted as a counterweight to suppression, repression, and the denigration of Humanity by those who wielded the sword.

Education became more and more a feature of the life of the average citizen and, while the body may be ruled, the minds of individuals were more and more open to inquiry, rational inquiry. The Mesopotamian view of man in the universe was pessimistic, one of alienation and subjugation, seeing no escape from the evils of life and no answer to the quest about its meaning. Only the Egyptians and the Hebrews viewed life from a spiritual perspective. The Greeks built upon these ideas and introduced a worldly optimism which gave virility to the religious viewpoint by demanding individual duty and responsibility to the affairs of the world from each individual. Let it not be supposed that each Sumerian, Egyptian, Hebrew, and Greek lived his life daily under the ideal of his or her civilization. These were the underpinnings which differentiated one from the other and influenced their world view and perhaps their conduct.

The movement toward an efficient world empire would be brought to fruition by the Romans. Roman rule would be tempered by Greek thought, but it would not be until the Renaissance of the fifteenth and sixteenth centuries that civilization would provide, once again, a basis for the renewal of intellectual culture and inquiry to which we hold fast today. Roman reforms took centuries, while Greek reforms took only years. In many ways Greek civilization still exists, the dreams of world influence have been fulfilled and lives on in all who ask "Why?" and who retain a hope and a belief that there is an answer which can be discovered and understood by all.

Let us now go and march with the Romans.

Chapter 11
Romans

Almost simultaneously with the rise of the Greeks, the Latin tribe in Italy was founding its home base for world rule—the city of Rome. The history of the ancient Romans was to last for about 1,229 years, from the legendary founding of Rome in 753 B.C. to its fall in 476 A.D., that is from 2,753 years ago to 1,524 years ago. Slowly but steadily, Rome advanced upon the world as a lion stalks its prey. Resilient and more successful than her neighbors, Rome expanded her influence and domination of the world to eventually create an empire which stretched from England to the Persian Gulf, from the borders of Germany to include all of Egypt. All roads truly led to Rome.

The history of Rome is one of resiliency and transformation from a kingdom, to a republic, to an empire, to decay. In the 1,200 years of its existence, Rome at its height was the world, having absorbed by conquest all of the ancient civilizations and pushed forward and outward its control of previously uncharted lands. If the Greek contribution to civilization was mental and spiritual, then that of Rome was structural and practical. Their real genius was in conquering and ruling other people despite defeats and setbacks. Rome learned and came back to conquer through organization and determination. Roman advances in law and politics have been a major heritage of the Western world.

The old societies of the Middle East and of the Hellenistic world, engrossed in the pursuit of wealth and private comfort, were easy prey for the austere legions of Rome. Other peoples traversed the Mediterranean in search of commerce, of learning, of new homelands. The Romans came only as conquerors. Their consistent behavior was predicated on the fact that they knew no other way of life. Republican Rome (509 B.C.) was a paramilitary state, its citizenry was its army, and its chief religion was a fanatical belief in the Roman destiny to rule the world.

Political stability, a citizen's army which had a personal stake in victory, was far more effective than the opposing mercenary or slave armies. It was a superior military organization which organized, equipped, and trained the Roman legions, and the skillful treatment of conquered peoples which granted local control and partial citizenship insured Roman dominance until the last 250 years of its existence. The virtues of self-discipline and duty served it well until corruption and internal decay destroyed its strength.

Rome's greatest triumph rested on the bringing of peace, Pax Romana (31 B.C. TO A.D. 180), under the Roman sword. It ushered in a continuation of a second great Hellenistic age in which men could and did travel from one end of the Mediterranean world to the other without hindrance. The vast expansion of Roman rule overseas from 238 B.C. to A.D. 44 was motivated by the greed of the Roman aristocracy and made possible by the fanatical devotion of all the resources of Roman society to military pursuits. Internal dissensions in the Hellenistic kingdoms and Carthage in North Africa meant a lack of unity against Roman conquest.

By the third century A.D. rot had set in. From A.D. 235 to A.D. 285, the empire was afflicted with a severe case of succession trouble. The army began to choose the emperors and to murder them with monotonous regularity. Class warfare and the arrogance and venality of the high and low of the population slowly debilitated the martial fervor of Rome and its internal sense of justice and discipline. A breakdown in orderly government and imperial authority had occurred from which it never fully recovered. Rome's foes took advantage of it to breach the defenses, and local warlordism appeared in the absence of any firm or respected authority. Mental and physical stagnation set in as the government became more repressive and powerless to control events, and the population no longer served or, for that matter, had children out of disillusionment.

The decline of Rome encompassed but 200 years of its history but is a fascinating tale of evil and sadness, for in the last years of its life the old Rome faded away under barbarian encroachment and like a rotting fruit the internal decay became terminal.

Pessimism and alienation were engendered by the relatively static quality of Roman life, by the Roman failure to achieve an industrial revolution and, with it, that self-sustaining economic expansion which inspired optimism about the future of society and devotion to the public good. The empire split into a Latin West and a Greek East.

At the end for the Western Roman Empire in A.D. 476, the intellectual, economic, and political world bore little resemblance to the might and optimistic classicism of Augustan Rome, 27 B.C. At its peak during the reign of Caesar Augustus, Jesus Christ was born. His teachings, later institutionalized in the Catholic Church, would hold together a despairing populace and act as a counterweight and counterpoint to the collapse of Roman rule some 500 years after His death.

Rome left a legacy of law and efficiency but also a legacy of terrible agony, for the underlying doctrine of Rome was that might is right. The Roman effect upon the culture of the Western World almost demanded a spiritual balancing brought about by the Christian Church to alleviate the dark, materialistic side of Roman culture. The Colosseum was an architectural and engineering marvel, but slaughter was enacted within. The Roman Empire was the most harmonious and successful multiracial society the world has ever seen, and yet its foundation was the sword of the Legionnaire.

The order, discipline, and purposefulness of Rome, at its height, was a legacy much desired in the world after Rome fell. What followed was a Dark Age of ignorance and barbarism alleviated and rescued only after a long period by the triumph of Christianity with its startling message of loving one's enemies and that all men are the same in the mind of God. A very revolutionary thought then and now.

In A.D. 476 the German General Odoacer, Chief of the Heruli, was in charge of the now almost wholly German Roman Army. When he was snubbed by a puppet emperor, ironically one Romulus Augustus, Odoacer simply kicked him off the throne and made himself the emperor. No defending of the gates, no final spectacular battle, just a whimper and Rome of the West was gone. The ancient world was finished.

As a precursor of what was to be a continuation of the ongoing slide into chaos, Odoacer was subsequently murdered at a peace banquet in A.D. 493 by the Ostrogoth General Theodoric the Great. The murderous aspirants to power and their cohorts of retainers bridge the ages.

Chapter 12
Eastern History/Ancients and Civilizations

Just as humanity spread throughout the world, we should not think that all of history and all of human development was only happening in the Middle East and the West. Asia also has its history, and its advances were as great as those of the West.

North of the Roman Empire, extending from the English Channel to the far western reaches of Siberia lived tribes called barbarians by the civilizations of the South. As the Romans contended with Germanic tribes, so the Chinese and Indian civilizations battled with Aryans, Mongolians, and Huns. Internally and externally, the history of civilization at this time was a balance of fending off threats to disunity and harmony.

Both China and India emerged as the dominant civilizations of the East approximately 1,000 years after the emergence of the nations of Sumeria and Egypt. This is not to say that there were no Chinese or Indian civilizations but that, due to the nature of geography and records, the written history of their political existence does not begin until 2000 B.C. The art and literature of the East is as beautiful and as distinct as that of the West. The feats of engineering and of science were at times far advanced over their Western counterparts. The Great Wall of China, begun approximately in 300 B.C. and completed in A.D. 1600, stands as a work of 1,900 years and is a monumental testament to Chinese efficiency, determination, and engineering.

Paper was invented in China in the first century A.D. It was 400 years before knowledge of it reached Spain, another 200 years before it reached Germany, and 300 before it reached England in A.D. 1000. Gunpowder was invented in China in the eighth century A.D., 500 years before it appeared in Europe.

Since we are of the West, our study of history often gives us a slanted view implying that only the works of Westerners were of any importance. As stated, humanity had spread throughout the world, only geography separated the groups. The brain was the same, and parallel civilizations sprang up at nearly the same time. Our legacy and way of thinking of the world was founded in the Western experience, but that is not to say that the lessons of the East are not of value.

Let us now examine two of the more salient contributions to civilization made by China and India. Once again, after the armies have marched, the spiritual legacy remains.

Chapter 13
China and India

The main difference between East and West developed along attitudinal lines. The West moved toward a spirit of individualism while the East developed a more internalized attitude. In the fifth century B.C., Confucius, a wise Chinese scholar, left to mankind his ethical teachings of harmony and proper balance as fundamental to happiness and well-being. His thoughts have guided the way of life in China ever since, holding this vast nation through ages of difficulty. He pointed a way out of the chaos and gave order to a diverse land. He sought to call into existence the aristocratic man in order to produce the noble state. Decorum and self-restraint have become the universal tradition of one-quarter of humanity, all of this 550 years before the Birth of Christ.

At the same time, Buddha, a rich prince of India, propagated his view of detachment from the tribulations of the world. He directed people to seek a higher realm within themselves and to not be debased by the material aspects of the world.

The vast regions of Asia were, in general, ruled under heavy-handed, stagnant, autocratic systems in which the mass of the people were not participants but followers. Individual thought and expression became an internal concern setting the stage for the eventual explosiveness of the West upon the East. Despite the invasions of the Huns against the West from 300 B.C. to 1600 B.C., it was the Europeans who, with the might of their Industrial Revolution, subjugated India and China.

This inward-looking attitude brought about mental stagnation and an arrogance founded upon the accomplishments of the past. As Europe exploded outward in an orgy of discovery and adventure, the East observed and only muttered that it had seen all of this before and that it did not really matter. Their spirituality was perhaps less hypocritical than that of the West, for it was not hooked up to Hellenistic/Greek thought which saw perfection not only in the spiritual but in a combination of mind and body.

Neither Western rationality nor Eastern spirituality have proved to be the answer to existence as both have matching strengths and weaknesses. Neither has fully created a perfect society for all of its people and both are blemished with Humanity's unique ability not to follow to a conclusion any idealistic path.

Part IV

Middle Ages
Current base line date: A.D. 2000
Real time: 1,500 to 1,200 years ago
(A.D. 476 to A.D. 1450)

Chapter 14
After the Fall

With the collapse of Western Rome 1,524 years ago (A.D. 476), civilization in the Western area of the empire, particularly in Europe and the Mediterranean Basin, collapsed. The provinces of Rome were invaded by numerous barbaric tribes known collectively as the Barbarians or the Germans. They were fierce nomadic fighters given to drinking and gambling, as well as being a hardy people. They came because they were motivated by land due to over-population, booty, and adventure, as well as the comforts of the superior Roman civilization. For the next 1,000 years (A.D. 476 to A.D. 1450) Europe went through a period of collapse, numbness, and a slow rebirth back to a civilized state of affairs. The centralized power structure of Rome had collapsed to such an extent that chaos reigned as no warring tribe was sufficiently strong to exert a unifying effect. The common man descended into a brutal, primitive life made all the more wretched by a breakdown in sanitation and education.

Because of the great upheaval that began with the Germanic invasions, most historians see the mid-fifth century A.D. as the beginning of a distinct new era in the development of Western civilization. The scholars of the Italian Renaissance of the fifteenth century name the fifth century as a turning point in European history. These thinkers greatly admired classical culture and attempted to restore it to Europe in their time.

They saw the eight centuries following the fifth as a "middle age" of barbarism and superstition between two peaks of classical humanism and rationalism, the Greco-Roman world and the Italian Renaissance. The medieval era was regarded by the classicists as a "dark age" compared to the periods of dazzling brilliance which preceded and followed it. Today we divide this millennium as follows:

The Dark Ages: A.D. 476 to A.D. 950
High Middle Ages: A.D. 950 to about A.D. 1270
Late Middle Ages/Renaissance: A.D. 1270 to about A.D. 1450

Nonetheless, Western Europe was eventually to emerge as one of the most dynamic civilization in the history of the world, while the Eastern Empire in Byzantium and Islamic lands, with all of their initial advantage of wealth and learning, were to sink into ossification and decrepitude. This thousand-year period of European stagnation and ignorance was to be a preparation ground for a Europe that would dominate the world.

Throughout this entire Period the role of the Catholic Church cannot be ignored, for it served as a refuge for education and justice in a violent time. Sadly, the Church, due to its intervention in the world, lost its own way, leaving the European world spiritually divided to this day.

Let us now examine this strange period of time when Rome was no more and the Cross and the Sword contended for the souls and bodies of humanity.

Chapter 15
Dark Ages

After the fall of Rome, for the next 474 years (A.D. 476 to about A.D. 950), the times in the West were of decay, war, famine, and death. One tribe after another plunged into the remains of the Roman Empire, bringing about a dark age in which the lamp of civilization was nearly extinguished. Except for the part of the empire kept alive in the East behind the safe walls of Byzantium, the Roman world of stability and commerce and peace was no more. Legality totally broke down, and life was ruled by the sword.

Into the void of political instability and lost secular authority stepped the Roman Catholic Church which, until the 1500s, would hold sway as the moral force and legal authority binding the benumbed population into a semblance of order and justice. Mankind was guided for the next 1,000 years, not by a vision of earthly power and pleasure, but by a view of life as a travail, a horror, and an imperfection to be endured.

To aspire to a heavenly realm was far more of a reality than the blood, mud, and mayhem below. Art, sanitation, education, and intellectual inquiry were crushed under the onslaught of the barbarians. Outwardly besieged by Asian hordes and Moslems and inwardly betraying and slaughtering one another, the world wasn't a fit place to exist for the beleaguered Westerner.

The Christian Church, the Jews, the Moslems, and the Chinese, as well as the Eastern remnant of Rome kept the lamp lit as Europe's own candle underwent a profound dark night of chaos and despair. The times were rent by war among the many tribes, alliances with the Church, and ignorance and superstition.

By A.D. 800, the Church had installed a Frankish king called Charlemagne as the new Holy Roman Emperor. His reign at least brought a semblance of order under the tribe called the Franks and gave impetus to the setting up of governmental functions. Upon his death, possibly due to overeating, his Church-approved kingdom was split into three by his sons, thereby forming the lands of what was to become France, the Middle Kingdom, and Germany. Ever since, the borders between France and Germany have never been peaceful, but at least some form of territorial lines were now in effect, and the Church had started the Europeans onto the road of nationhood.

Life in Europe began to settle into the age of feudalism where land and hierarchy bound people to a routinized drudgery and a harsh loyalty to their lord. Though private wars still occurred, stability was slowly seeping back into the western lands.

Chapter 16
High Middle Ages

We shall now cover the 300-year period from A.D. 950 to about A.D. 1270. This age found the dust beginning to settle and a European identity slowly begin to emerge. The Catholic Church, despite it own lapses and moments of venality and corruption, continued to be a moral force guiding the affairs of men through a troubled world. Art, literature, and inquiry were beginning to bubble beneath the surface of the feudal, agriculturally-based societies. Life was no picnic for the average man and woman dominated by the Church and lords. Raised in ignorance and superstition, the journey was for the most part a travail to be endured in the hope of a paradise to come.

In the tenth century, Europe began to dig itself out of the miseries that had hit it as a finale to the Dark Ages' last 100 years from A.D. 850 to A.D. 950. This dreadful final 100 years included the final disintegration of the Frankish Empire, the destructive attacks of the fierce Norsemen and Hungarians, the reduction of society to its lowest common denominator of sheer brutal survival. There arose the isolated self-sufficient manor and the fragmentation of political rule and law down to the level of one's local robber baron.

A Saxon King, Otto the Great, defeated the Hungarians and was quickly backed by the Catholic Church, which was wise enough to allow for the continuing rise of sectional powers which began the formation of France, England, Italy, and Germany. Europe was in preparation to be reborn. It was to be a long pregnancy.

Though the entire period of the Middle Ages was to us a time of warfare and religious obsession coupled with a general breakdown in law, it should not be construed that these were times of medieval gloom and doom. From our own pompous position of the twentieth century we may view those times as gloomy, when nobody had any fun, everybody

45

wore hair shirts, and human nature was despised as all prepared for the next world and couldn't wait to be relieved of this one. One does not have to look far into the Middle Ages, particularly the High Middle Ages, to find such things as a frank sexuality, boisterous and bawdy songs and stories, erotic poetry, fun poked at the clergy, drinking songs, and wild music to which the people danced.

Indeed, this is all part of the picture which some nineteenth-century romantics saw as the "merrie Olde England" and "sensual French" of olden times. One may find this openness to life in the romance of chivalry, the love lyrics of Provence, the fabliaux and farces of the people. There were travelling jugglers and minstrels; fairs, festivals, and dances; and numerous religious holidays. Sunday was a merry day. Memories of pagan festivities mingled with these Christian holidays. Contrary to widespread opinion, one of the chief legacies from medieval times is fun: simple, open, and earthy.

The High Middle Ages were a colorful, romantic, glorious time, even if life was still short and somewhat brutal. The final schism between the Roman and Eastern/Greek Orthodox Church occurred in A.D. 1054 and continues to this day. William, the Duke of Normandy, successfully invaded England; towns rose throughout Europe; Moslems were pushed back into Spain; and the Great Crusades began to liberate the Holy Land in A.D. 1096. Four of these adventurous episodes were launched and were to last until A.D. 1204.

The Crusades not only engaged the power of the Moslems and kept them in check from overrunning Europe but served to decrease the overpopulation that had occurred in Europe in the eleventh century due to stability and better farming methods. They also served to expose Europe to the new knowledge of the East and the old forgotten knowledge of the ancient world. In general, they served to open the European mind to the world beyond their forests and villages and to instill a pride in what was seen as the legacy of the European/Roman/Greek mind. Travel serves a broadening purpose and perhaps never on a more grand scale than the Crusades.

The Crusades also gave voice to the deep spiritual roots of the European culture. This mixture of deep spiritualism and spiritual vulgarity was vividly displayed in the magnificent building of houses of worship, the great cathedrals of gothic design. Europe was relearning its ability to create artistic building which expressed the inner thoughts of the people.

The Roman law was rediscovered and parliaments representing various powered factions began to meet and address their concerns. Universities were established to disseminate the new knowledge from the East.

Nations of Europe were taking form, the revival of economic life was moving briskly, cities were emerging, manners were becoming more civilized, and education was leaving the monastery and moving out among the people. All in all, it was a time of bubbling adolescent growth, adventure, and sensuality. Economic, political, and intellectual growth alongside artistic and architectural growth were being discovered and were setting the stage for a foundation for the later intellectual flowering known as the Renaissance.

Certainly a brilliant age of growth and advancement was refined in the Late Middle Ages. Nonetheless, there is an entrancing mixture of romance, religion, idealism, fanaticism, and scholarship that still attracts the Western mind to this refounding of what makes us a bit of the Yahoo—an inquiring brash mind with a touch of piety. We are what we are.

Chapter 17
Late Middle Ages

The years from A.D. 1270 to about A.D. 1450 saw Europe flower intellectually and militarily into a pattern of aggressive thinking which was to
make this area of the Earth dominant up to present-day in the affairs of
humanity. As misery begot religious fervor which led to the Great Crusades, so the Crusades begot the introduction of knowledge of the world
and learning which led to inquiry which led to further knowledge, and
so on to our present times. This period was called the Renaissance, though
its roots belong to the High Middle Ages; this time was the flowering
and rebirth of Western strength and international growth.

While the East and the Middle East were content, if not smug, in the
level of their civilization compared to the backward barbarians of Europe, the Europeans were about to discover their roots and their self-
confidence. They were going to make up for lost time with a vengeance.

The input of new ideas, increased trade and improved methods of
farming resulted in a population increase, which in turn provided many
willing new hands and minds for new endeavors. No longer was every-
one bound to the land for now the cities beckoned. "How are you going
to keep them down on the farm, after they have seen Jerusalem?", may
well have been a song as the soldiers returned from the Crusades.

Though peace, art, trade, and education marked the beginning of this
time and were not to be put back in the bottle of a dark age, this period
ended on a sour note due to the very changes taking place which threatened the "powers that be," the Papacy and the nobility. Not only was the
old hierarchy being questioned and threatened, but increasing violence
and a wide variety of natural disasters added to the social dislocation
and unrest.

Fluctuations in trade brought upon by the manipulations of money and
the Moslem conquest of the Eastern Roman Empire in A.D. 1453 caused
a Great Depression which lasted for nearly 175 years. The historian

J. Hiuzinga, who has studied the mood of these times, speaks of a "sombre melancholy" and "immense sadness" in the sermons, chronicles, poems, and documents of the period. Peasant revolts occurred in Germany, France, and in England. Princes argued and disobeyed the Church. The Protestant Reformation broke the solidarity of Christendom and ended the dream of a universal government under the direction of God's representatives. England and France engaged in a Hundred Years War from A.D. 1337 to A.D. 1453 to contest the remains of feudal holdings in France held by Norman lords, and France was to experience years of sporadic, localized famine in the 1400s.

The winters turned colder and the dreaded Black Death (bubonic plague) ripped through Europe starting in about A.D. 1350 and killing at least 25 percent of the population; in some cities and districts as many as 50 percent died. The plague was much more severe in cities than in the countryside, but its psychological impact coupled with weather changes and Moslem encroachment penetrated all of society. No one was safe from the disease, and once it was contracted, a horrible and painful death was almost a certainty. The dead and dying lay in the streets and waysides, abandoned by frightened friends and relatives. The effect of this devastating epidemic was reinforced by severe recurrences several times over the next fifty years.

Nonetheless, the Renaissance took hold and was to begin to change the attitude of humanity from group and class thinking to individual expression. Since neither one's Lord nor Church could protect and guide one through the morass of earthly existence, it was best to use one's own mind for one had only one life to lose and to live.

The Renaissance took hold despite the general malaise in finances and social and political life, and indeed it took hold as a reaction to the problems outlined herein. Leonardo de Vinci painted the *Mona Lisa* in A.D. 1509, Michelangelo began painting the Sistine Chapel in A.D. 1508, and Machiavelli's *The Prince* was printed in A.D. 1532. Individual thinkers would no longer be suppressed or repressed by the class system or by their times. Critical thinking was to lead us into the modern age. Individuals were interested in the literature, art, and ideas of classical (Roman/Greek) culture, which emphasized the importance of individual human beings and life on earth. This optimistic belief attracted many people and as the times worsened the individual struck out more and more on his own and gave less credence to the so-called rulers.

This impetus of chaos and independent inquiry, an almost schizophrenic mentality, gave its fullest expression in the age of European expansion and discovery. Inquiring minds wanted to know what was the true nature of the Earth and what was out there for the pickings. Europe had become too small for the minds of its best thinkers. Humanity was thinking more and more of the future with optimism, despite the ugliness of the particular present.

Come, there is a ship waiting.

Part V

European Expansion and World Discovery
Current base line date: A.D. 2000
Real time: 550 to 300 years ago
(A.D. 1450 to A.D. 1700)

Chapter 18
Far-Flung Empires/Colonies and Subjugation

By the end of the fifteenth century, the economic depression of the late Middle Ages was over, and the European economy began an upswing which lasted until the early part of the eighteenth century. In general, both population and prices rose for the greater part of the period from A.D. 1450 to about A.D. 1715. The general economic improvement was accompanied by an expansion of economic horizons for the sixteenth and seventeenth centuries and constituted the first great age of European geographical expansion and colonization.

Due to scientific advances such as the compass (from China), more accurate maps, improved rudders and sails, and the astrolabe, the sailors were ready. The Crusades and the Renaissance had provided the scholarly knowledge that the Earth was most likely round. The Greeks knew it to be so; the Norsemen had sailed to Greenland and North America as early as A.D. 1000 but seemed to have made no big deal about it; Marco Polo's account of his travels to China at the end of the thirteenth century stimulated a great interest in the Far East. All added considerably to geographic knowledge.

In A.D. 1418, Prince Henry the Navigator of Portugal began his explorations to India via African excursions. In 1488, Bartholomew Diaz reached the southernmost tip of Africa. In 1498, Vasco Da Gama sailed to India. In 1492, Christopher Columbus sailing for Spain journeyed westward hoping to run into Asia but instead found a new world. By A.D. 1519, Magellan sailed around the world, though he spent most of the journey in a pickle barrel due to his being killed by natives in the Philippines.

Other nations followed, and the race was on to explore and exploit the new-found routes, land, and peoples. Other cultures in China, India, and the Middle East had the capacity but not the hunger as did the

Europeans. As a result, Europe was to rapidly outstrip these moribund societies and to exploit those from which it had learned. Exploration brought exploitation, and this brought wealth, power, imperialism, and capitalism. No longer could one let the world go by; for the world was now reachable.

The establishment of colonies led to the need for labor which led to slavery. Unable to make the native Americans work as hard as they wished, the Spanish introduced Black Slavery to the New World. New lands would mean new freedoms but also new miseries for those not in positions to defend themselves or set ways of life. Many of the cultures dominated by the Europeans were "set" and perhaps even contented. There is no shame in this. The tragedy is that their ways were disregarded and destroyed. Wealth for the few was to be built on the misery of many and the hopes of many seeking a better world.

The exploration of the world during this period not only was to foster an increase in nationalism but was to create new wars, new nations, and new ways of living. By the beginning of the 1700s, we had left behind the medieval mind-set and had embarked upon our modern age.

We should keep in mind that what passes for advancement is often not viewed from a moral or spiritual view point. For example, the indifference and insensitivity of Europeans to non-Europeans was one of the more unfortunate, as well as most enduring legacies of the early modern era. Money, power, and status, whether on an individual or national level, should not be seen just as growth, for often there is a sad underside to the gaining of these perceived virtues. What was an advance for Europe marked the end of life for an untold number of innocent human beings. The forces unleashed by European expansion were to nearly consume Europe as well within the next 250 years. Progress has a price.

Part VI

Modern Age
Current base line date: A.D. 2000
Real time: 300 years ago to current
base line date (A.D. 1700 to present)

Chapter 19
Europe Reigns/Industrial Revolution

From A.D. 1750 to about A.D. 1914, the Western world went through a period of optimistic advancement called the Enlightenment. This was an intellectual movement of the late seventeenth and eighteenth centuries fostered by the scientific and personal attitudes of the sixteenth and early seventeenth centuries. It was an optimistic creed, one that felt that all human problems could be solved by the correct use of human reason. Philosophers and scientists were almost indistinguishable in the use of their intellectual powers to use induction, of finding facts by examining many individual instances and then framing them as a general rule from these experiments.

Financially, militarily, and artistically societies took the temper of their intellectual leaders and applied it to the mundane matters of running the world. The mind of Man had replaced the Mind of God as the arbitrator of human endeavor. The events and trends mentioned in the last chapter played their part: relative peace, war as a set piece game rather than the past general mayhem, political stability, and economic growth. The English made advances in personal freedoms. Overseas expansion and monarchs who played by the same rules all added to this optimistic view. It was widely believed that, despite intermittent warfare over colonies and strips of land, history and society were in capable hands and that progress would be steady.

Scientific discoveries about the nature of the universe, the American and French Revolutions, and the general trend towards greater power and participation for the common people added to the liberality and contentious spirit of the times. Education and awareness would see a general rise in the consciousness of the whole human race. Abuses and repressive actions of the past would eventually be removed. Slavery as such was abandoned as a formal institution by 1865. Progress was always slow and often bloody in its coming, but it nonetheless could not be resisted. Nations would bloody each other's noses in wars of petty imperialism, but in general it was agreed that a balance of power was preferable for all to enjoy the advancements which the human mind would provide.

By the early 1700s the Industrial Revolution had begun in England and was to spread rapidly throughout Europe and the Americas. This revolution made Europe wealthier, more populous, and in possession of tools of commerce, navigation, and war such as enabled her to thrust herself on the outer world of Asia and Africa. It also brought her a whole new range of problems and new ideas. New methods of producing iron, new sources of power, advances in transportation, advances in communication, and the expansion of banking while bringing economic progress for many also cost huge dislocations in the traditional habits of society. These times raged with arguments about capitalism, socialism, economic policy, and the welfare of the working masses.

Though new and greater quantities of goods could now be produced, the spiritual and traditional ties to the land were being wrenched asunder. Ideologies of liberalism, socialism, nationalism, and democracy abounded attempting to make sense of a world suddenly speeded up with change in lifestyles, roles, and living conditions. Progress in medicine, science, and commerce sadly again appeared to go hand in hand with misery. The masses suffered and only begrudgingly won their crumbs at the table of progress.

Wherever one looks, the century of the Enlightenment shows dynamic aspects, along with grave disturbances, which were to be a hallmark right up to 1914 when the problem and Achilles' heel of secularism was found to be as flawed as the Middle Ages's dependence on the Roman Catholic Church. Revolution and more revolution, political change, class conflict, and cultural crisis abounded. As the legacy of the French Revolution worked itself out in increasing national identity, Europe turned in the direction of political liberalism and democracy. It became a fixed belief in the Western world that science, technology, and popular enlightenment were combining to produce a new era of the human race. But there were many who were deeply concerned about the loss of values and of cultural stability in a race for wealth, power, and position, as well as the rise of mass democracy which often appeared to be but a form of mass manipulation. These gnawing doubts continued on until the coming debacle of 1914.

We should note that our time frames are becoming shorter and more intense. They but reflect the general "speeding up" in the pace of world events brought about by quicker communications which leads to more ideas which leads to a quickening pace of change. Change itself was to prove a weak answer to humanity's search for a meaning to life. Change often brought freedom but at the price of disharmony. It would seem that despite universal advances in mechanics and scientific discoveries, the human race more and more was feeling as if it lived in a tower of Babel.

Chapter 20
European Suicide/Return of Barbarism

The ability of humans to manipulate and control their environment led to a need for resources, hopefully at a cheap price. Since this could not be guaranteed, imperialism became the answer and the road to power, status, adventure, and survival of the fittest. The advances of the seventeenth, eighteenth, and nineteenth centuries and the rise of nationalism and many other-isms of thought took on an almost religious fervor as humanity now sought a reason to live in biological success, by being at the top of the heap for one's life span. The glory of man had indeed replaced the glory of God.

The nations which pursued an active imperialism in the latter part of the nineteenth century were Great Britain, France, Germany, Italy, the United States, Belgium, the Netherlands, and Japan. The game had been going on for some 200 years between most of these nations, but it was now about to reach a horrible climax during the 20th century. Large-scale production, rivalry in armament, and technological advances were not only leading to material comfort and betterment but to wars of destruction on a scale never seen before.

The results of imperialism were a mixed bag, but a careful review shows that the disadvantages in the long run far outweighed the advantages. Western culture was further spread throughout the world, and law and order were encouraged in many backwards areas. The ideal of Alexander the Great to spread one's culture and to unify the world was still a strong one, but it still came down to "My culture is better than your culture." Imperialism aided economic growth in both Europe and its colonies, but far too frequently upon the backs of exploited peoples who shared very little in the wealth generated by their sweat. While sanitation, transportation, healthcare, and increases in production were introduced to many primitive areas, the price was usually political and economic domination. The worst aspect was that the increased imperialistic rivalries increased European tensions and helped to facilitate World War I in 1914-1918.

Searching for incidents that could have caused the war to end all wars can become almost a game, and the chronological limits on it can be unlimited. Suffice it to say that at this point in time the past rivalries had reached a crescendo point made all the more dangerous by new weapons such as poison gas, the submarine, the machine gun, and huge artillery. With the assassination of Archduke Francis Ferdinand, heir to the Austro-Hungarian throne, at a place in the Balkans called Sarajevo, Serbia, the psychological readiness for war came into play between the Allies (France, England, Russia, and later Italy) and the Central Powers of Germany and Austria-Hungary. This was a World War fought not just by the main European powers but eventually calling in their client states from around the world.

The war makes for good reading, but the results were a horror for 10 million lost their lives and some 20 million were maimed in mind and body. In terms of property destroyed this was over 175 billion dollars. The impact of the anguish and disruption of the war cannot be measured. Europe became psychologically scarred as a result. The peace was such that it left Europe holding its collective breath before the next round.

Communism surfaced as the rule in a collapsed Russia. The Russian people were to suffer a dark night of internal terror and a horrific invasion by the German Nazis in the coming Second World War. Some 23 million Russians were to die over the next fifty years from internal repression.

A wounded Western world was shoved over the edge with the Great Depression which ran its devastating course in the capitalist countries. Beginning in 1929 with the American stock market crash, economic depression seeped through Europe and by 1932 reached a stage which made it the worst of all international economic collapses, bringing suffering and misery to millions of people and setting the stage for the rise of dictatorships in Germany, Italy, Hungary, Rumania, Russia, and Japan. People worldwide began to lose faith in reason, democracy, and capitalism. The progressive systems simply were not working due to the fear, dislocation, and damage of the First World War. Capitalism must also share the blame for the human condition of selfishness and greed were at play, as usual, in manmade institutions. In 1930, 1 percent of the population controlled approximately 39 percent of the wealth within the U.S.A. The average person was once again living with a serf's mentality of normality under onerous economic conditions.

Germany, Italy, and Japan attempted to take on the world in an Axis of conquest and very nearly succeeded. The Second World War unofficially began in 1931 with Japan's invasion of China and officially in September in 1939 with Nazi Germany's invasion of Poland. The war raged around the world until August 1945 with the Axis powers defeated by an Allied crusade.

The statistics were staggering—some 15 million soldiers and 45 million civilians perished. Damages were estimated at 4 trillion dollars. Subsequent estimates have raised the death toll to 100 million. The war left the world more confused and divided than did the First World War.

The attitude of human rationalism had proven to be just an attitude. Genocide was committed on a massive scale, and the horror of technological madness paled to insignificance the depredations of the Ancients or the violence of primitive peoples. The age of the barbarian had returned with a vengeance to a smug European consciousness. Butchery had been achieved on a grand scale by an educated people with a superior culture. The best and brightest of world civilizations had committed atrocities upon their fellow human beings on an unprecedented scale. Progress, education, and enlightenment were seen to be but a thin veneer. There had been a great hidden well-spring of hatred, anger, hypocrisy, and evil beneath the surface of the world's greatest civilizations.

The energy of the civilizations had spent themselves in an orgy of bloodletting made all the worse by the sophisticated blandishments of propaganda, and the ability to mass produce weaponry despite the cost to national treasures and human lives. All nations were quite willing to spend their blood, to maim and kill large portions of their populations, in an irrational drive to claim victory at any price. The result was a war of no mercy and the sanctioned murder, the sanctioned destruction, of millions of non-combatants. Atrocities and the denigration of the individual to national purposes became logical, rational expediencies. To not participate in this thinking was to die on a national and individual level. Death reigned.

Chapter 21
Cold War

For the next 45 years, from 1945 to 1989, the world suffered through a wasteful period of military tension between the democratic/capitalistic nations led by the United States and the communist nations led by Russia. The destruction of lives and of property were only the external symbols of the damage and displacement wrought by the Second World War. The nation-state system of Europe had been destroyed, old countries and powers either disappeared or were weakened, and the coming of the Atomic Age and the destruction of two Japanese cities by single bombs had changed the outlook of the world.

The states of the world found themselves, even as the peace was being made and an international organization created, split into two rival camps, the Soviet and the Western blocs. Gradually, as the new nations of Africa and Asia emerged, a third bloc emerged, the Neutral or Non-Aligned nations. The world had become dangerously bi-polar, uneasy and constantly on the verge of war with little if any real progress in solving the problems left over from past wars or new ones.

Russia and the United States fought surrogate wars but never came fully to blows as both feared the mutual destruction of their nuclear arsenals. Two nations alone now had the capacity to literally destroy human life upon the planet. Both spent their fortunes on more and more sophisticated systems of destruction while also pursuing policies of space exploration to the moon and beyond. Money became no object in proving to the world which nation was superior. Both suffered internally as a result. Despite feats of accomplishment in science and in space, their internal structures became mutually rotten, corrupted, and hypocritical.

As both nations poured their fortunes and their moral worthiness into their client states and their military-industrial complexes, the two prime instigators of the Second World War, Japan and Germany, built up their education and commercial systems insuring for themselves strong economies as their old victors slowly hemorrhaged in a display of pompous military posturing. The results of their actions were to steal from both America and Russia the fruits of their worthy victory in the Second World War.

By 1989, due to internal rot and the crushing of its own people, Russia as the Soviet Union abandoned the Cold War almost unilaterally, and the U.S.A., now suffering its own internal decline, also began to cut back. The world breathed a sigh of relief for the anxiety of a full-scale nuclear war between Russia and America appeared to have passed. The damage to the world in wasted resources and blighted cities had already been done. That which might have created a more sane, productive, moral, beautiful world had been squandered in the pursuit of war preparedness. One is reminded of the old Roman saying: "Beware of a great victory, for it is the beginning of your defeat."

Such was the case with the main victors of the Second World War, Russia and America. Once allied against the Germans and the Japanese, they had become enemies for the next forty-four years only to see those that they had conquered rise from the ashes stronger than ever. History ignored in the pursuit of power and position.

One more sad tale of the inability of humankind to think through clearly and to fear and prefer to wage war than to extend the hand. Rationalism, realpolitik, was missing an element of spirituality and of love. It would appear that education and position merely were tools to garner and stay in power and privilege at any cost. The People were not served but were harnessed to serve and go along with policies which did little but limit their lives.

Just as the purely religious view foundered, so has the rationale for they both require something of the other to work. Religion without Rationalism becomes superstition and intellectually insulting, and Rationalism without a spiritual aspect merely loses its way in its own posturing and ego leading us back to a more sophisticated form of barbarism, as the concentration camps of the world so aptly demonstrated in the bloody twentieth century.

Part VII

**The Past, Present, and Future
Current base line date: A view from
the twentieth century or two thousand years
since the birth of Christ**

Chapter 22
Lessons Learned: Contention of the Emotional, Intellectual, and Spiritual

We have seen both horror and nobility, optimism and despair. The story of human life aside from moral judgements and one's preference for optimism or pessimism is as written by Hume: "To see the human race, from the beginning of time, pass as it were in review before us...what spectacle can be imagined as so magnificent, so various, so interesting?" From the dimmest mists of prehistory to the last age of man and woman, we may be near its end or only at its infancy. All we know is that it is an amazing story.

To learn lessons from history is an old axiom which is perhaps quite meaningless given the nature of the rise and fall of each generation. The lessons are surely there, but the human race within each generation considers itself unique even as they repeat the old patterns of power, mating, status, warfare, and hope. Do they listen? Do children really listen to their parents or take note of the experiences of their elders? It would seem that most individuals within a generation prefer to learn through their own, falsely believed individualized, unparalleled and unrivaled existence? Language, locations, and nationalities change, yet there is a sense of the same game being played by different players. The contentions, the search for justice, the manipulations, the guarded arrangements seem to wend their way into each generation's passing.

The horrible violence of our own latest century is a mournful reproach to the ideas of progress and betterment with which it was ushered in. Progress has been seen to lead not necessarily to a betterment but to a misuse, violence, and destruction on a merely more efficient scale. While the world is even more closely knit as far as transportation and communication, the relationships between nations and individuals are no better nor worse than before. Masses still suffer in mind and body. People suffer loneliness, love is not found. Massacres and economic dislocations continue in our time.

So far as can be judged, the experiment of humans can hardly be said to be a success. It has produced some extraordinary things, but the possibility of its destroying itself cannot, even after this passage of time, be dismissed. It is clearly a story of noble struggles, defeats, and occasional triumphs amid much suffering, tragedy, and injustice, of the rise and fall of empires and of people. A great deal of activity has come to pass in which the indomitable will of humanity to build a better world, a civilization, is evident.

New generations arise to question and to change the "truths" of prior beliefs. This may lead to a continuation of the status quo, a reaffirmation, new growth, or an apathetic stagnation and decay. Nothing is guaranteed over the span of time. The drive, moral fiber, or worth of one generation may not be inherited or even be recognizable in their grandchildren.

Is it all simply, "A tale told by an idiot, full of sound and fury, signifying nothing?" Is there a direction and a culmination of the journey? We do not know of other life as of this writing. We may well be the highest form so far developed, and therefore it is good to keep in mind how short a time we have. We have worked our way upon this oasis called Earth and at what a price in blood, tears, joy, hope, and love. What is it to be a human? What is it to be happy to be alive? Are the Rich any happier that the Poor? Do wealth and gadgets bestow wisdom and wholeness? Our advanced civilizations seem to require a great consumption of drugs, alcohol, tranquilizers, consumerism, pornography, and banal entertainment to function, serve as a reward, or to merely get through the unacceptable reality of the daily grind. It would appear that the price of civilization in regimentation, social conformity, competitiveness, and thwarted biological drives can be rather high in psychological disorientation.

Not only is greater adaptation to change demanded of the population, but our innate legacy of genetic drives is often ignored at our peril. We function. We are fed. We wonder why we feel ill at ease, and why so much of our daily lives seems to be lacking in spontaneity and joy, except on the screen or via a drug. We are a questioning species even when we can not fully articulate our discomfiture. Again we are attempting to look for a direction as the old ways have led into blind alleys. Our Age of Science is ongoing and in competition with New Age thinking which hearkens back to nature and the spiritual rhythms of the universe.

It does appear that as a species we are not wholly rational nor as highly evolved as our idealistic platitudes would lead us to believe. We can talk the talk but have not quite mastered the daily walk. Saints among us are rare and usually end up martyred in one form or another. Compromising is our easy way out, and when that fails, we go for the sword or some other form of physical or psychological violence, fairly quickly too, I might add.

It does appear that we are in need of balance and harmony—particularly as a result of our capacity to destroy our own planet by weapons or pollution. The Greeks believed in a balance of Mind, Body, and Spirit. Since the time of the Egyptians, this hidden dimension has played a role in the journey of humanity. Our intellect should not be insulted by the spiritual aspect of being human for it can be seen that working on its own it becomes but a slave to the emotions of the material body seeking power, pleasure, and security, usually at the expense and suffering of our fellow beings. Far, far too often our intellects have been used for venal, selfish purposes to serve our greed, our egos, our mating schemes.

Without the Triad of Mind, Body, and Spirit, our best, most noble ideals become unfulfilled, our existence one of false platitudes, our civilizations illogical and hypocritical. "Know thyself; Moderation in all things; Love one another," the lessons are there, the signs are up. Only our ignorance, our fearful flesh, and our difficulty in loving holds us back from building a paradise on this oasis of a planet and from finding a meaning to existence beyond our stomachs, beyond our deaths.

Each civilization and each human consciousness has, despite their flaws and failures, had an idealization of self worth. For each there was that "one bright, shining moment" when their energies and intents were fully engaged and expressed the power within their mind, body and spirit. Decline, rot, and betrayal set in when one of the three became either weak or too dominant. Without a harmony of mind, body and higher will then the age old pattern of reoccuring disillusionment and loss will afflict one passing generation to the next.

Caravans aren't meant to wander aimlessly in circles, along beaten paths, but are to arrive at a destination—and so are we.

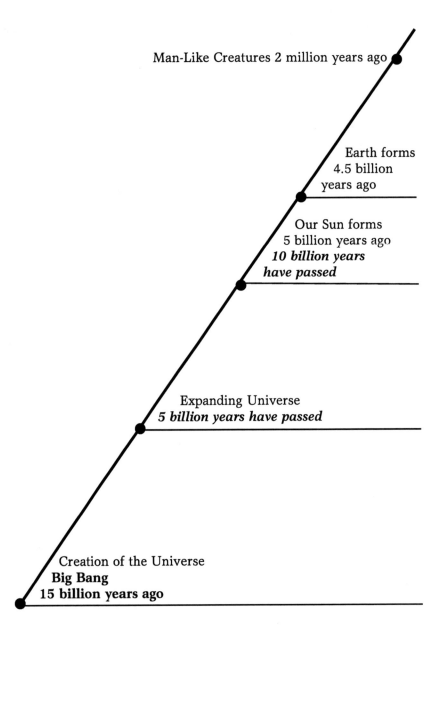

Man-Like Creatures 2 million years ago

Earth forms
4.5 billion
years ago

Our Sun forms
5 billion years ago
**10 billion years
have passed**

Expanding Universe
5 billion years have passed

Creation of the Universe
Big Bang
15 billion years ago

Time Line

No Time	The Unknown
Big Bang/Time, Matter, Energy	15-20 billion years ago
Sun	5 billion years ago
Earth	4.5 billion years ago
One-Celled Life	3.5 billion years ago
Life on Land	600 million years ago
Dinosaurs	225 million years ago
Ape-Men	12 million years ago
First Man-Like Creatures	2 million years ago
First Fully Human/Neanderthal	100 thousand years ago
First Homo Sapien/Cro-Magnon	60 thousand years ago
Homo Sapien/Modern Man	35 thousand years ago
First Civilizations	6 thousand years ago
Sumerians/Egyptians**	
Greek Olympiad	2,776 years ago
Rome Founded	2,753 years ago
Birth of Christ	2,000 years ago
Crusades	904 years ago
Christopher Columbus	508 years ago
World War I	82 years ago
World War II	55 years ago
Landing on the Moon	31 years ago
End of the Cold War	11 years ago
The Future	Till the End of Time

Sumerians/Egyptians** (Civilizations of the Fertile Crescent)

Egyptian Early Kingdom 3000-2700 B.C.
Egyptian Middle Kingdom 2000-1800 B.C.
Egyptian New Kingdom 1546-712 B.C.

Assyrians 850-722 B.C.
Babylonians 605-538 B.C.
Persians 539-333 B.C.

Book Review

Riverview Teacher Makes World History Understandable

By BARBARA DERBYSHIRE

A lack of what he calls "time concept" is the major obstacle to understanding the gift of history, says Robert John-Patrick Berkeley of Bourne. To remedy that situation, he has written *Once Upon A Time: A Brief History of All That Was, Is, and Will Be as Far as We Are Able to Comprehend.*

Mr. Berkeley's book was published this spring by Dorrance Publishing Co. and has been doing well in this country and in England.

In seven short chapters totaling 69 pages, Mr. Berkeley has encapsulated the major events of the past into a highly readable form that helps us see history as a map of time so we can understand how and why we ended up in the here and now.

Mr. Berkeley wrote in the preface to *Once Upon a Time* that "our actions and decisions should be informed ones, informed, inspired, and forewarned by the experiences of our fellow human beings who, though they are of the past, have journeyed ahead of us on the road of existence."

As a teacher, Mr. Berkeley said he realized that students didn't understand the continuity of history, the cause and effect of events. "They were getting history piecemeal and were never putting it all together," Mr. Berkeley said in a recent telephone interview.

The result of this piecemeal education, he said, is a profound ignorance of history. "The flow of time must be understandable, otherwise confusion sets in followed by apathy and subsequent ignorance, prejudice and intolerance," he said in *Once Upon a Time.*

The book is based on a compilation of notes he made while teaching junior high and high school history. He currently teaches at Riverview School in Sandwich, where he is also head dormitory counselor.

Although he wrote the book "out of need for students," he said it is aimed at adults as well.

His interest in seeing the whole view of history began when he was stationed in Europe. "They'd just come out of World War II, and they'd looked into a bit of hell," he said. "Their view of history is more realistic than ours. It isn't all the whoopie-do, feel-good history that our students are learning. The European view is not necessarily negative, but it is more realistic about human nature."

Mr. Berkeley's enthusiasm for history continues with his participation in the 12th Massachusetts Infantry, a group of Civil War re-enactors. "We get in touch with the past," he said. "We get to relive history, and when you live it, it's a whole different ballgame. You have a keen appreciation of what drove those people."

Once Upon a Time, which sells for $8, will be available at the Market Bookshop in Falmouth, and it can be ordered from any bookstore. It is published by Dorrance Publishing Company Inc., 634 Smithfield Street, Pittsburgh, Pennsylvania 15222.